Fashion Design Illustration

Children

This book is due for return by the last date shown above.
To avoid paying fines please renew or return promptly.

Portsmouth
CITY COUNCIL
LEISURE SERVICE   CL-1

Fashion Design Illustration

Children

Patrick John Ireland

B.T. BATSFORD LTD · LONDON

First published 1995
Reprinted 1998

© Patrick John Ireland 1995

Typeset by Servis Filmsetting Ltd,
Manchester

and printed in Great Britain by
Butler & Tanner Ltd, Frome and London

Published by

B.T. Batsford Ltd
583 Fulham Road
London SW6 5BY

www.batsford.com

A CIP catalogue record for this book is
available from the British Library

ISBN 0 7134 6624 3

Acknowledgements

Images on pages 34, 36 and 42 courtesy of
United Colors of Benetton.

Photograph on page 2 by Rainer Usselmann.

I would like to extend my thanks to the
Bournemouth College of Art and Design,
Berkshire College of Art, the Cordwainer's
College, London and all the students and
lecturers in the many colleges and workshops
I have worked with for their encouragement
in producing this book.

Thanks also to Richard Reynolds and Martina
Stansbie, my editors at B. T. Batsford.

CONTENTS

The aim of this book is to help students to design and illustrate children's and teenage fashions. A designer should possess a general awareness of fashion and a sound knowledge of fabrics and the use of colour. He or she should be capable of finding inspiration from many different sources, and be able to develop these ideas to create original designs. A sound knowledge of both pattern-cutting and the methods of making up garments is also a necessary requirement.

Initially, many students of design find it difficult to express their ideas on paper and need help in acquiring good fashion drawing techniques. This book is arranged in sections to cover different stages in the fashion drawing process as it relates to children and teenagers. The first section starts by setting out the proportions of a child and shows how these change as the child develops. By working from the figure charts provided, you can relate these proportions to your design. You can develop your design skills through creating and utilizing figure templates. Beginners will find it helpful to copy or trace them directly from this book and then work on them with the aid of semi-transparent paper or a light box.

The fashion designer needs to develop a style of drawing that is clear, fluent and adaptable. Costume and life classes are extremely helpful in this and should be attended if at all possible. The method of figure drawing shown will enable you to master a number of sketched poses, from which you can create attractive and functional fashion design ideas for different age groups. Suggested exercises, areas of research and projects are given in the different sections of the book.

Drawing children

It is important to be aware of the changing proportions of the growing child when drawing and designing for different age groups. The exercises in this book will help you to sketch the figure accurately, working out the correct proportions according to age. The beginner will find it helpful to work from the charts illustrated, constructing the figure by calculating the number of heads that would fit into the length of the body. You also have to remember that the size of the head and the length of arms, legs and feet will alter according to age.

If possible, practise sketching from life, observing children's attitudes – the way in which they move, walk, skip and climb. It is difficult to draw children in a set pose as they are not very patient models. It is better to make quick sketches from life and develop them later.

Design sketches and illustrations for children's and teenage fashions are often produced using a stylized drawing technique. Some are very highly stylized like a cartoon. The style of drawing will reflect the image you wish to project.

Examples using a variety of techniques such as pen and ink, pencils, felt pens, markers, paints and pastels are given throughout the book.

There are three stages of drawing when designing:

1   **Design development**
In the earliest stages of developing a design, sketches should be fairly rough, exploring and experimenting with the many possibilities within each idea or theme. These groups of drawings are known as design

development sheets. They should indicate design ideas, showing both the front and back views of the garments illustrated. The types of fabric, pattern and texture should also be suggested, perhaps with a sample fabric attached to the sheet. Notes can be added to convey any details not shown in the sketch.

2 Production drawings

When a design has been approved, a sample garment will be requested. The production team will need a specification sheet and a production drawing in order to show details of seam and dart placement, cut and any other proposed style features.

3 Presentation drawings

Presentation drawings are used to present a collection of design ideas to a client. They should be finished drawings which project the intended fashion image of the designs. This means that careful thought should be given not only to the drawing of the garments, but also to the pose of the figures, hairstyles and accessories in order to achieve an attractive overall effect. Different ways of presenting the work should also be developed, taking into account the colour and pattern of the fabrics. The designer should become adept at using colour in presentation drawings, to suggest the effects of pattern and texture. The colours of the fabrics chosen for a design should always be accurately represented in presentation drawings.

Layout and presentation effects

Presentation drawings are used on several occasions: when showing design ideas to clients, entering competitions, setting up displays, as well as for portfolio work for interviews and assessments.

Many different techniques may be used for the presentation of work. The layout and mounting need to be carefully considered. Photographs, sketches and decorative effects can be introduced, often as a backdrop to complement the design drawing. The photocopier can also be a valuable tool. However you should take care never to let the presentation of your work overpower the design drawing itself. Examples of different presentation drawings are given in the later sections of the book.

The baby

A new-born baby is nearly four times the height of its head. The head is proportionally large, with the torso being about one and a half times its size.

A new baby has pouches under the eyes and little bulges over them. The nose is very short and the upper lip is long. The arms and legs are diminutive and the hands are small and doubled up into the fist.

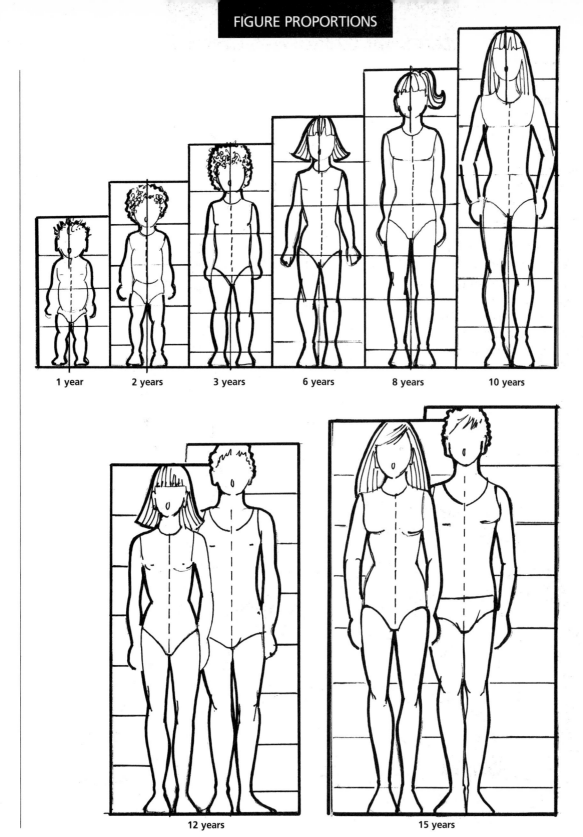

1 year 2 years 3 years 6 years 8 years 10 years

12 years

15 years

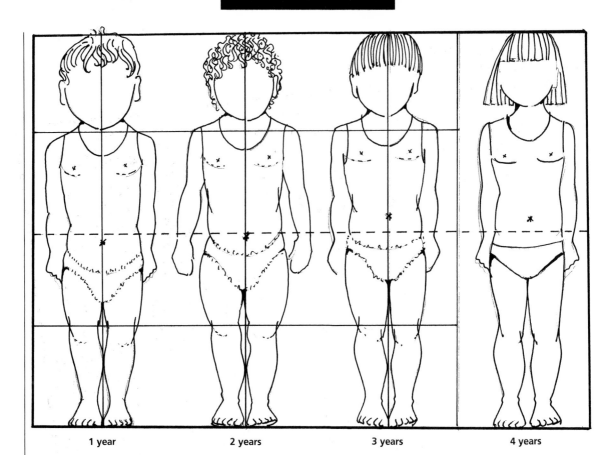

1 year   2 years   3 years   4 years

During the early stages of growth, the infant's limbs are proportionally short, with the upper limbs at first longer than the lower.

The middle line of the body is above the navel; after two years it is on the navel; after this it is above this point.

At three years:
Note the stylized technique used in the presentation of the beach outfits. The proportions have been observed from the figure chart.

5 years (5 heads)

9 years (6 heads)

12 years (6 heads)

16 years (7 heads)

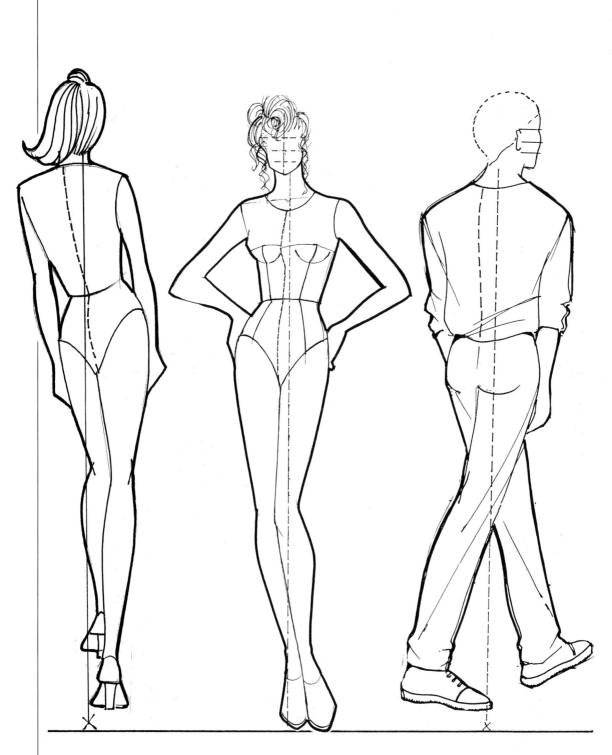

18–25 years

18–25 years

The technique of drawing garments over a template with the aid of a light box or semi-transparent paper can be used to develop design ideas. Work around the outline of the figure to create your own design, remembering to take into account the type of fabric

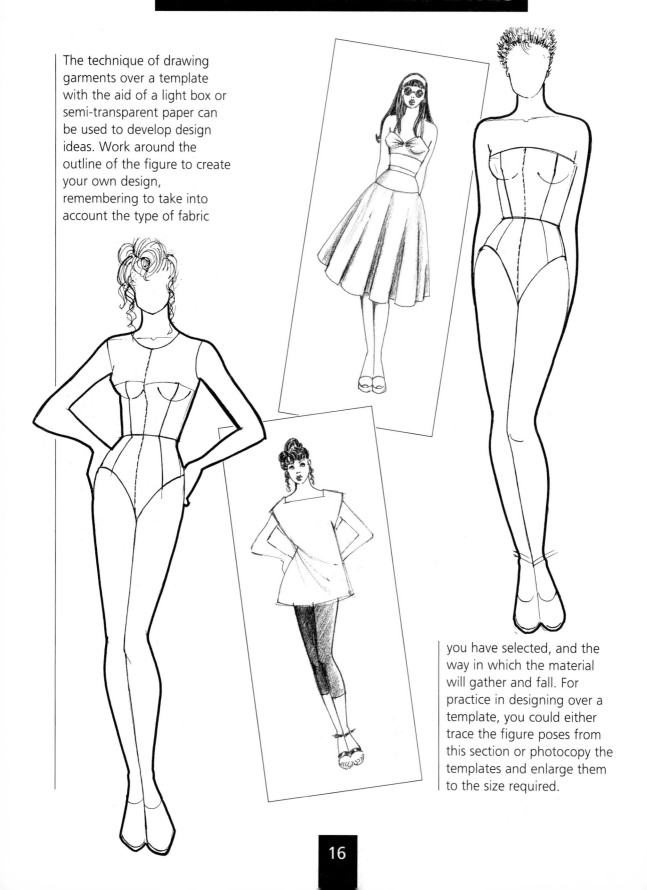

you have selected, and the way in which the material will gather and fall. For practice in designing over a template, you could either trace the figure poses from this section or photocopy the templates and enlarge them to the size required.

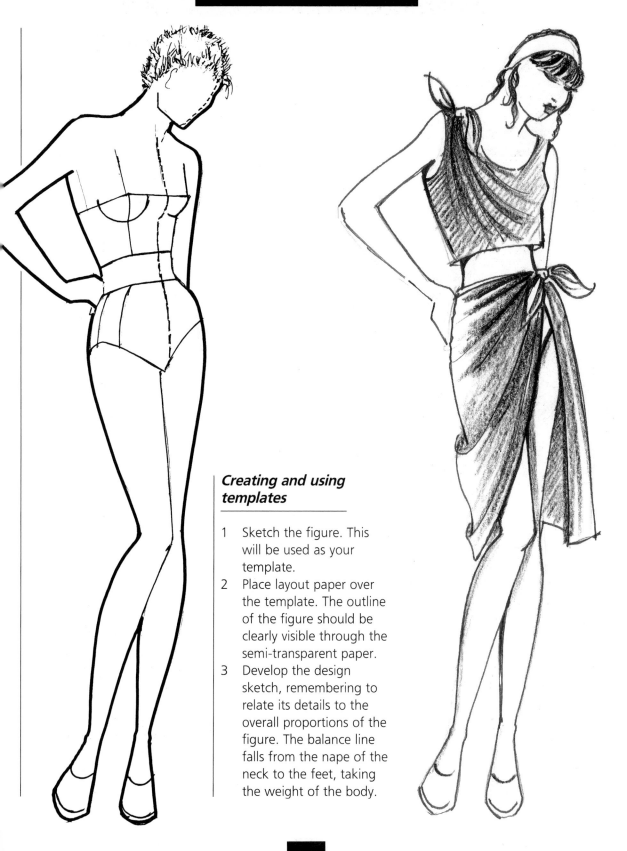

Creating and using templates

1   Sketch the figure. This will be used as your template.
2   Place layout paper over the template. The outline of the figure should be clearly visible through the semi-transparent paper.
3   Develop the design sketch, remembering to relate its details to the overall proportions of the figure. The balance line falls from the nape of the neck to the feet, taking the weight of the body.

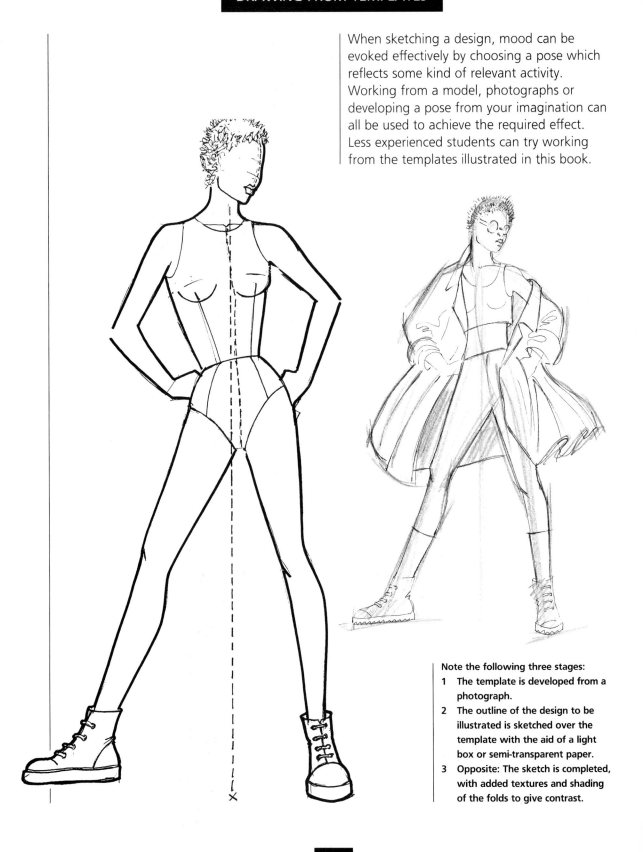

When sketching a design, mood can be evoked effectively by choosing a pose which reflects some kind of relevant activity. Working from a model, photographs or developing a pose from your imagination can all be used to achieve the required effect. Less experienced students can try working from the templates illustrated in this book.

Note the following three stages:

1 The template is developed from a photograph.
2 The outline of the design to be illustrated is sketched over the template with the aid of a light box or semi-transparent paper.
3 Opposite: The sketch is completed, with added textures and shading of the folds to give contrast.

The balance line falls from the nape of the neck to the floor, indicating how the weight of the body is supported. The attitude of the pose and the swing of the coat give movement to the sketch and contribute to its general mood.

This sketch was produced in three stages, working from a template.

1. Firstly, a template of the figure was drawn, working from the basic proportions.
2. The layout paper was placed over the figure and the design sketched.
3. The sketch was developed using a pale grey marker pen and a soft black pencil for shading. The details were suggested with a fine Pilot Hi-Techpoint pen. The shading on one side of the figure was made darker to give extra dimension to the sketch.

When working on a study of a baby, it is a good idea to make plenty of rough sketches while the subject is asleep.

When the baby learns to sit up, it becomes more interesting to draw. It will provide a variety of entertaining poses and attitudes as it tries to balance. At about a year old, the baby begins to crawl, fall down and toddle.

This sketch was produced quickly
using a soft black pencil, observing
the overall shape and movement of
the pose.

Practise creating new poses by working from the life mode. When sketching children, you have to work with speed as they are not very patient and quickly become restless. As an exercise, try sketching quick poses of two to five minutes, using a free line technique.

Experiment with different media, using a selection of pencils, charcoal, inks, marker pens or watercolour paints.

Keep a sketchbook and make quick sketches of children in different attitudes when playing, running, skipping or jumping. You only need to draw a few lines to suggest the pose or action.

Your construction will be based on a few simple lines. A semicircle or oval gives the shape of the head. Establish the position of the spine with a simple line. This will give you the basis of the pose.

Indicate the tilt of the head, the angle of the shoulders and the action of the arms and legs. A few lines in the right position are enough to convey the pose.

This quick sketch made with a soft pencil indicates clearly the movement of the two figures. It was developed with a Derwent sketching HB pencil, and the textured effect was achieved by placing canvas under the paper and rubbing the pencil over the surface.

A drawing produced with a soft black Carbothello pencil. When working with this pencil, you need to use a fixative spray in order to protect the sketch from smudging. One side of the figure is emphasized to give extra dimension to the sketch.

As a useful exercise, try sketching quick poses from life over two to five minutes using a very free line technique.

1 Start with a pale grey magic marker pen to indicate the figures, and add details by working into the tone with a soft pencil.

2 This kind of sketch may be developed by using a light box or layout paper.

Most fashion design courses have special classes allocated to life drawing and fashion drawing. Practise creating new poses by working from the life model. Experiment using different media and various grades of paper, and work on large and small drawings using both very free and more controlled techniques.

The previous quick sketch, developed with the use of a light box.

The textured effect representing the fabric was achieved by placing canvas under the paper and rubbing a soft pencil over the surface. Details were added with a Pentel fine line drawing pen; note the thicker line used to add interest.

Stylized drawings

Stylized drawings are often exaggerated in their proportions. They should have a sense of fun. The heads are often increased in size, with cartoon faces. The feet are large, and the shoes emphasized.

Certain features of the garment are singled out in order to dramatize them; for instance, the fullness of a skirt, very full sleeves or an outsize collar could be highlighted.

It is important to make the most of the features of the design, as the drawing has to complement its subject.

In drawing this pose, the solid figures have been exaggerated to give emphasis to the sporty fashion image. The use of stylized techniques introduces different line values and textures; for instance, note the use of two thicknesses of black pen. The textured effect which gives tone to the coat and boots is created by placing canvas under the paper and rubbing a soft pencil over the surface.

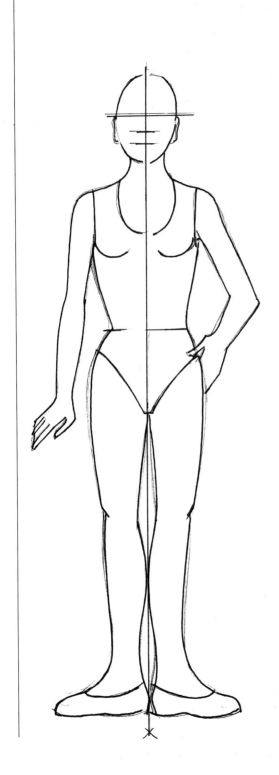

Drawing in three stages:

1 A simple template was developed from the figure chart.

2 The design was worked on over the template using a light box or semi-transparent paper. The sketch was produced with a black fine line pen.

3 A wax crayon was used to create the effect of hair. To complete the image, a cool grey magic marker pen was used for tonal effect. The print for the T-shirt was reduced on the photocopy machine and placed on the front of the shirt with spray mount. The folds in the T-shirt were suggested with white paint.

If a model is not available to draw from, it is useful to work from pictures from magazines or to take photographs with your camera. Select poses that are suitable for illustrating clothes.

Photographs may be used for
1 developing figure templates to be used when designing.
2 improving your drawing skills when a model is not available. Work from photographs observing the style details and folds of the fabric.
3 inspiration. Change and adapt the pose to create new templates.

1. Select a photograph to sketch, considering the pose and details of the garment.
2. Sketch in a free style, preferably using a soft 3B pencil. Note the balance and proportions of the figure.
3. Complete the sketch by working over the original with layout paper or use the light box to develop a more stylized drawing. Experiment with different media from pen and ink to pastels and watercolour.

Stylized drawings from a photograph, produced with pencil and an Artline 200 fine 04 pen.

Developing figure poses

Select a photograph and analyse the pose, considering the centre front line of the figure and the balance line of the leg, taking the weight of the figure.

Sketch the figure from the photograph a number of times, changing the position of the arms and legs, and so developing different poses from the one photograph.

Place layout paper over your sketches and develop variations of the pose as illustrated.

Proportions

The length of the head at birth is about half that of an adult's. From the front view, the child's head appears much squarer. Because the bone structure of the face is smaller, the centre of the head is above the eyes. The head of the child will grow more in length than in breadth.

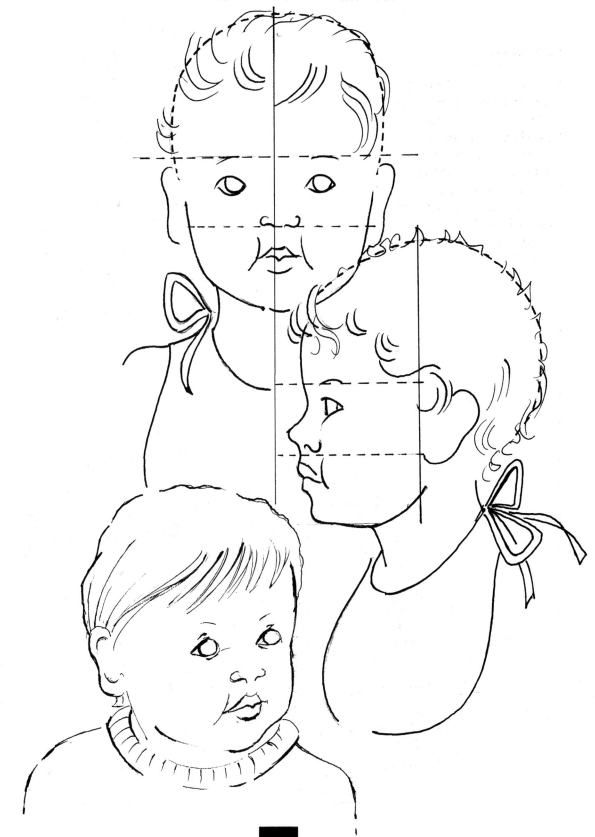

Note how the proportions of the head alter as the child becomes older. The face narrows and the eyes appear smaller as the face grows larger.

Work from photographs of children and sketch from life if you are able to find a model who will sit still. Experiment with different techniques and make stylized sketches of different expressions.

A selection of sketches drawn from photographs. The faces have been produced with a soft black pencil, combined with a fine line pen for details. Soft shading has been used on the hair and face.

It is helpful to work from photographs when a model is not available. Select faces of different age groups from photographs you have taken or from magazines.

For fashion sketches you should stylize and simplify the drawings. Adapt the features and hairstyles to gain the effect you require for your illustration.

The hat is an important accessory when creating a total fashion image. The designer will start by working on a theme, producing a selection of design sketches to develop their ideas. From these sketches, the designs are created in the millinery workroom. The foundation fabrics and materials are draped and modelled on a wooden millinery block.

The hat is drawn in two stages. It is helpful first to construct a drawing with a few guidelines sketched in lightly with a pencil, indicating the position of the hat in relation to the head.

A selection of some of the basic styles from which many variations can be worked. When designing, keep the sketches simple. They would be developed using different illustrative techniques if they were intended for presentation.

The shoe is an important accessory to a fashion image. Until you have the confidence to draw shoes in detail, it is a good idea simply to suggest them in your fashion sketches with a few lines.

Keep a sketchbook of styles, noting the details of new shapes, toes and heels. Keep abreast of current trends in shoe collections by studying the displays in shop windows and photographs in fashion magazines and observing colour trends and any new materials or trimmings used.

As a useful exercise, sketch shoes from different angles, selecting different styles and experimenting with a range of techniques to achieve a variety of effects.

1 Outline the shape of the shoe.
2 Note the centre front line to help balance the details.

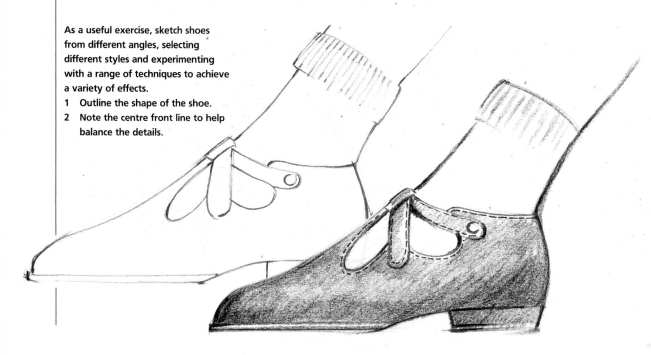

This sketch was developed in three stages using a black pencil.

1 The basic shape was sketched, paying attention to the centre front line for balance.

2 The details were added, whilst taking account of the proportions of the shoe.

3 The finished sketch, complete with details of stitching and shading.

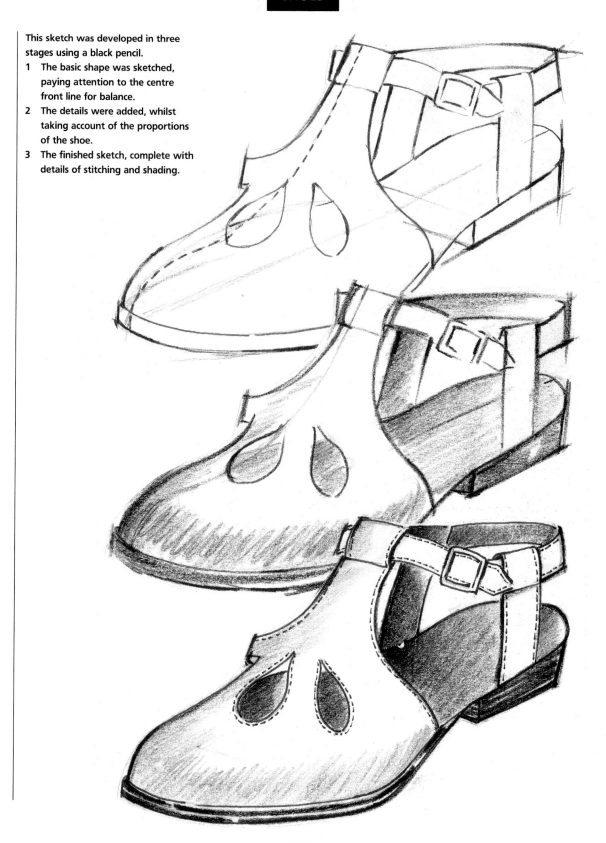

When sketching shoes, note the general shape and proportions first, and the way in which the shoe or boot has been constructed. Then work in stages, adding tone and colour to complete the sketch.

Start with the shape of the shoe, then develop the details of seam placement, lacing and stitching. Experiment with different media using pencils, paints and marker pens or a combination of these materials.

Drawing shoes from a variety of angles will help considerably when fashion sketching.

When displaying work to a client or presenting work for assessment at college, it is effective to illustrate a design on a board, suggesting the environment in which it would be worn.

SPRING SUMMER

SPRING SUMMER

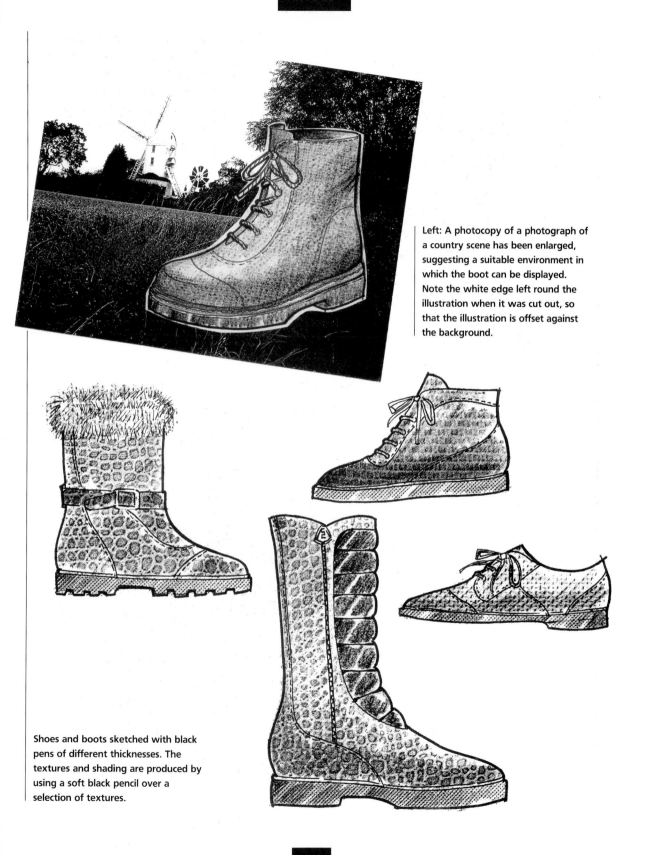

Left: A photocopy of a photograph of a country scene has been enlarged, suggesting a suitable environment in which the boot can be displayed. Note the white edge left round the illustration when it was cut out, so that the illustration is offset against the background.

Shoes and boots sketched with black pens of different thicknesses. The textures and shading are produced by using a soft black pencil over a selection of textures.

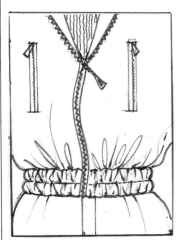

It is good practice to make detailed drawings of fashion details, observing the proportions and construction of pockets, collars, fasteners, pleats and sleeves.

Keep a sketchbook for this purpose noting any new design feature you may have designed or seen.

The drawstring is used effectively on many areas of a garment, such as the hems of jackets, blouses, necklines, sleeves and trousers. A cord is inserted in the casing or hem to pull an area of fullness together. The cord could be piping, braid or rouleau.

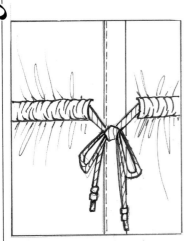

Drawing Fashion Details

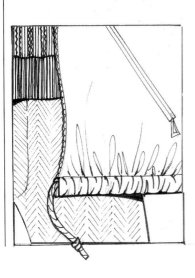

A tuck is a fold of fabric, either used as a decorative feature or for shaping. Tucks are even in width and stitched in groups. The effects vary according to the thickness of the fabric, its texture and its pattern.

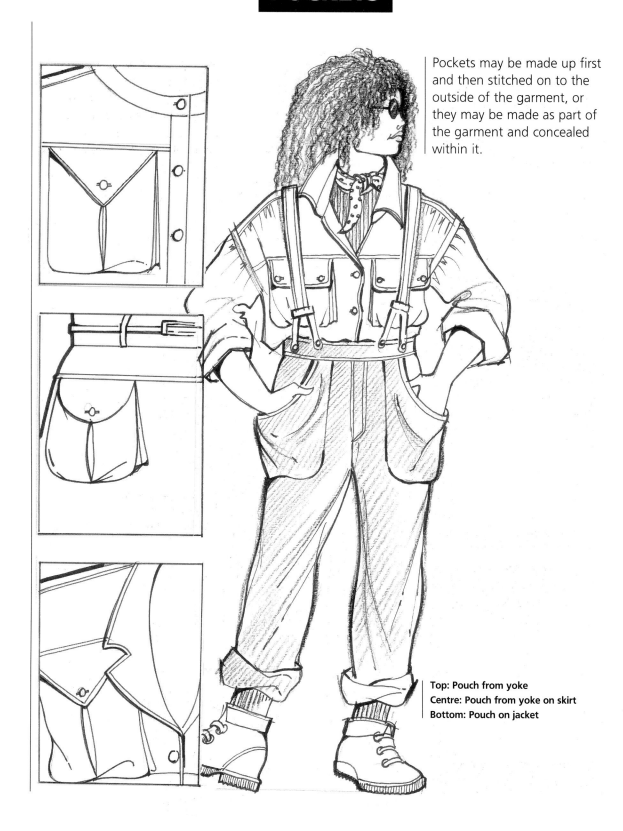

Pockets may be made up first and then stitched on to the outside of the garment, or they may be made as part of the garment and concealed within it.

Top: Pouch from yoke
Centre: Pouch from yoke on skirt
Bottom: Pouch on jacket

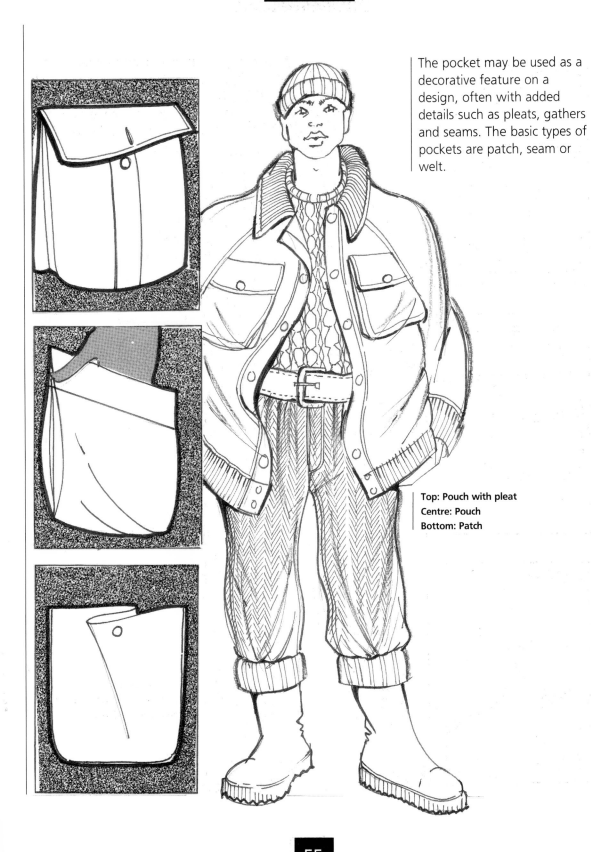

The pocket may be used as a decorative feature on a design, often with added details such as pleats, gathers and seams. The basic types of pockets are patch, seam or welt.

Top: Pouch with pleat
Centre: Pouch
Bottom: Patch

Collar designs are based on three basic styles: flat, roll and stand. They may be attached to the neckline, detached or convertible. The weight and texture of the fabric used for the designs will give different effects, and this should be carefully considered when producing design sketches. Many variations can be developed from these basic styles.

Sailor collar

Flat collar

Tailored collar

Stand collar

Collar with stand

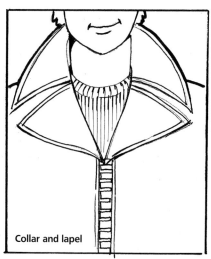

Collar and lapel

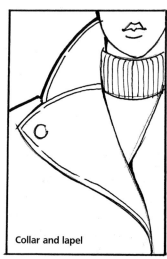

Collar and lapel

Variations of the set in sleeve

There are many variations of sleeve, but they are all based on three basic styles: set in, raglan and kimono. Different effects are achieved by adding cuffs, gathers, pleats, tucks and variations in the cutting.

From left to right: Raglan sleeve; Set in sleeve; Dropped shoulder line; Kimono sleeve

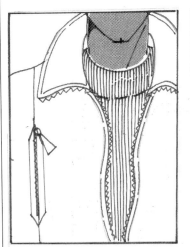

Zips are made in different widths and lengths from either nylon or metal. In addition to its function as a fastener, the zip has become a fashion detail used on many designs as a decorative feature.

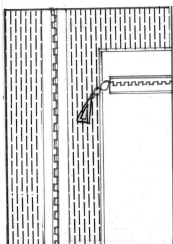

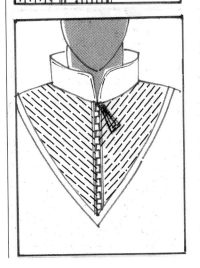

The three different types of basic pleat are the knife pleat, the box pleat and the inverted pleat. A pleat is a fold of fabric, and may be added to a design by allowing extra fabric and then folding it into place.

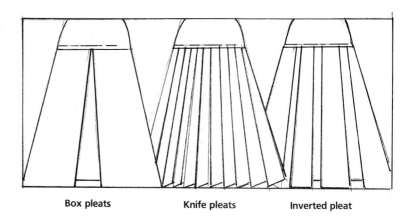

Box pleats   Knife pleats   Inverted pleat

Knife pleat

Box pleat

Full soft gathered folds

The fabric determines the amount of fullness that a flounce or frill will take. A flounce is cut from two circles. It is fully flared at the hem but keeps a smooth fitting line at the point at which it is attached to the garment.

Gathers occur where the fullness of the fabric is gathered into a seam. The effect will vary depending on the fabric used. When the fabric is draped on the bias cut, it will create draped folds.

Top left to right: Tiered gathers; Draped effects
Bottom left to right: Full gathers; Gathers; Gathers on hem of skirt

Textured and patterned effects can be developed with the aid of a selection of materials such as canvas, fabric, embossed paper or net. By placing a lightweight paper such a layout paper on the textured material and rubbing over the surface with a soft pencil, a textured impression is created on the paper.

It is useful to collect a folder of interesting textures for use when illustrating. Experiment with different pencils to achieve the effect you require.

Drawings produced using this technique.

You can achieve varying effects by using different media. Experiment with pens, paints, crayons, pencils, felt pens and markers. On the following pages, I have suggested some of the effects that you may obtain.

It is not always necessary to reproduce the pattern on your sketch in every detail; perhaps simply suggest it on one side of the figure. It is very useful to indicate the cut of the material by showing the pattern on the cross.

As an experiment, reproduce a sketch in outline on the photocopy machine a number of times and develop different patterns and textures on the copies.

Watercolour and wax crayon

Watercolour

Marker pens and pencils

Left: Experiment with patterns and textures in your sketchbook. Work from a variety of materials, suggesting tweed, checks, fur and leather.

Right: A completed presentation drawing, showing the use of textured effects produced by placing materials under the paper and rubbing the surface with soft coloured pencils. The thick black line round the figure was produced with a felt tip Pentel pen.

Opposite: Experiment with different line values when suggesting fur, folds and knitted textures. The surface textures have been achieved by placing a selection of canvas textures under the paper and rubbing a soft pencil over the surface.

A quick sketch made from life and developed afterwards to illustrate a sporty casual garment. The pose has been selected to project the right image, note especially the movement of the pose and the position of the feet. Careful attention has been given to all the details – the hood, boots and the elasticated drawstring waistband.

The completed sketch was produced with a black Stabilo pencil for shading and a hard black pencil for the details. The trousers were textured with a wax crayon.

Techniques and Presentation

Watercolour may be bought as a solid tablet or as a paste in a tube, and can be thinned with water. Paintboxes of different sizes are also available.

Unless you are using good quality paper, it should be stretched. If this is not done, the paper will react to the water, cockle and distort the work.

Opposite: Completed design drawing ready for presentation
Below: Templates sketched from the imagination.
Top right: sketch produced with a fine line pen in black over the templates.
Bottom right: Watercolour washes added in a free style leaving areas of white.

Above: Sketch produced from model using a pale grey marker pen and 2B pencil.

Right: Line drawing produced on light box with a fine Pilot Hi-Techpoint V7 pen.

Opposite: Finished sketch, with a soft lead pencil used for representing textures.

A large selection of pencils is available in different thicknesses from hard to soft. The choice of paper and its texture is important depending on the effect required. For instance, a tough textured paper is needed for a tweed effect and a smooth surface for a soft draped silk.

The pressure of the pencil gives a darker tone when shading. It is advantageous to have a selection of pencils when working, some sharpened to a fine point and others with a softer point for shading.

A pattern was added to these finished drawings. To create this effect, the actual fabric was first photocopied and reduced to the scale of the drawings. The required shape was outlined against the sketch, cut out and applied to the finished drawings.

The details of seams, folds and pockets were added with a fine black pen.

This pose was developed from a
photograph and stylized. The sketch
was completed with a Pentel pen and
a patterned fabric was photocopied,
reduced to scale and added to the
drawing.

Opposite: A presentation board illustrating the use of collage. The sketch has been stylized and produced with Stabilo soft colour pencils and a fine line pen for details. Textured effects have been used on the boots and a photocopy has been made of the fabric and reduced to scale for the garment.

These drawings were developed from imagination. Note the poses and the balance line. The sketches were produced with a fine black pen, and wax crayon was used for the hair and leggings. The striped T-shirt was created through the use of collage.

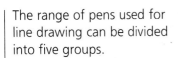

The range of pens used for line drawing can be divided into five groups.

1   technical pens
2   plastic tip pens
3   ball point pens
4   roller pens
5   felt tip pens

New types are being produced constantly. Experiment with pens and combine different line values in one drawing. The card or paper to be used has to be considered carefully, as the surface will affect the line value.

A drawing in two stages using different line values. The thick black line round the figure gives the finishing touch to this technique.

Note the two stages of this sketch, which was developed from a model.

1 The subject was quickly sketched in pencil, using 3B for the soft marks outlining the pose and 2B for details.

2 Opposite: The sketch was developed using a black charcoal pencil and sprayed with a fixative.

When design sketching, the mood of the design can be evoked effectively by choosing a pose which reflects some kind of relevant activity such as skipping, dancing, skiing or athletics.

Different methods may be used to achieve the required effect. Work from a model, photographs or develop a pose from your imagination.

This sketch was developed over a template. Note the balance line from the nape of the neck to the floor, indicating how the weight of the body is supported evenly on both feet. The swing of the hair and movement of the garments contribute to the general mood of the sketch.

The final sketch combines a line drawing with a collage effect for the top and a thick black felt pen for the trousers.

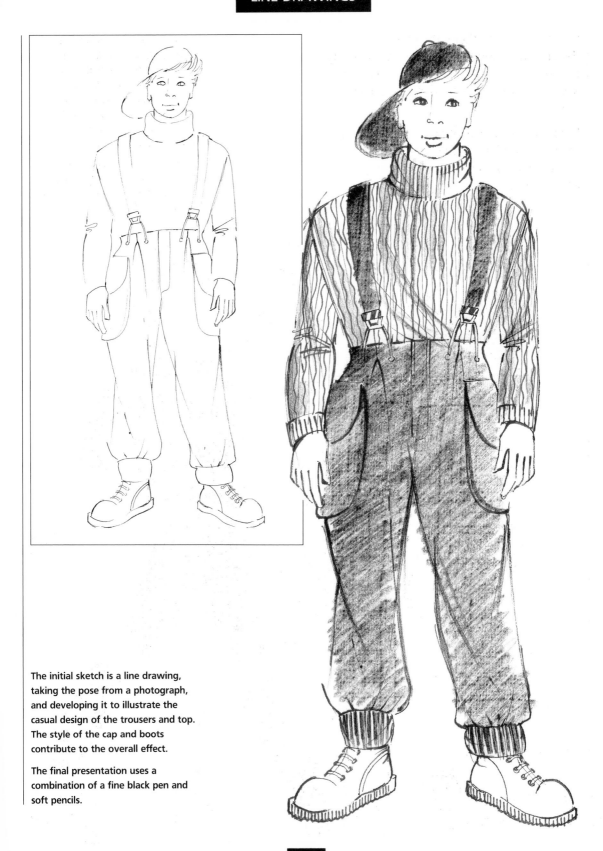

The initial sketch is a line drawing, taking the pose from a photograph, and developing it to illustrate the casual design of the trousers and top. The style of the cap and boots contribute to the overall effect.

The final presentation uses a combination of a fine black pen and soft pencils.

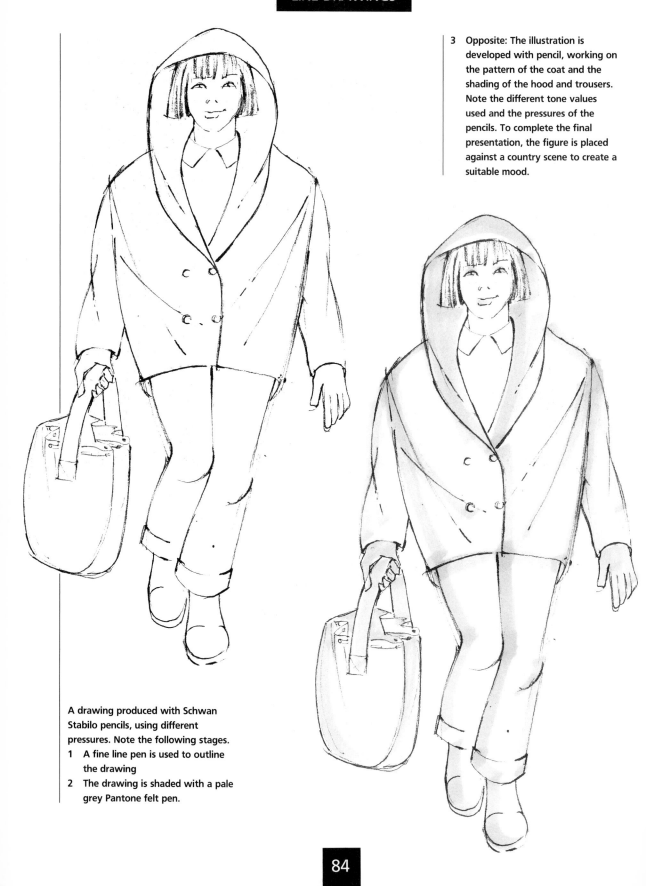

3 Opposite: The illustration is developed with pencil, working on the pattern of the coat and the shading of the hood and trousers. Note the different tone values used and the pressures of the pencils. To complete the final presentation, the figure is placed against a country scene to create a suitable mood.

A drawing produced with Schwan Stabilo pencils, using different pressures. Note the following stages.

1 A fine line pen is used to outline the drawing

2 The drawing is shaded with a pale grey Pantone felt pen.

These drawings were produced in line with a Pentel fine drawing pen. The pattern and tone were added with a Pantone marker pen. Note the accessories – bags, hats and lightweight canvas boots – introduced to complete the look. Again, the photograph in the background adds to the mood.

Opposite: These line presentation drawings are sketched with a 04 fine Artline pen. Note the figures chosen to illustrate this sporty casual image. The background picture was selected to suggest the summer holiday mood.

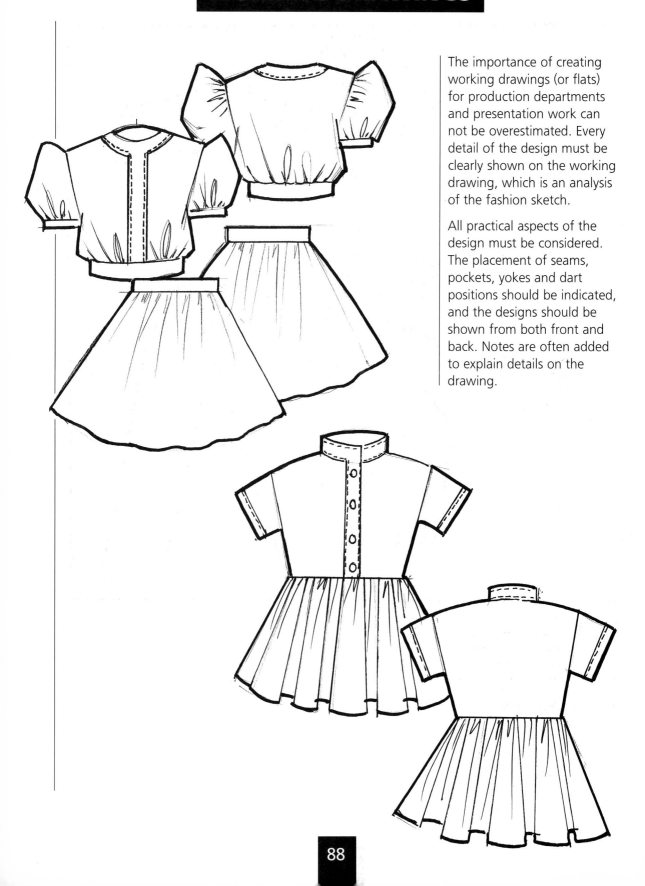

The importance of creating working drawings (or flats) for production departments and presentation work can not be overestimated. Every detail of the design must be clearly shown on the working drawing, which is an analysis of the fashion sketch.

All practical aspects of the design must be considered. The placement of seams, pockets, yokes and dart positions should be indicated, and the designs should be shown from both front and back. Notes are often added to explain details on the drawing.

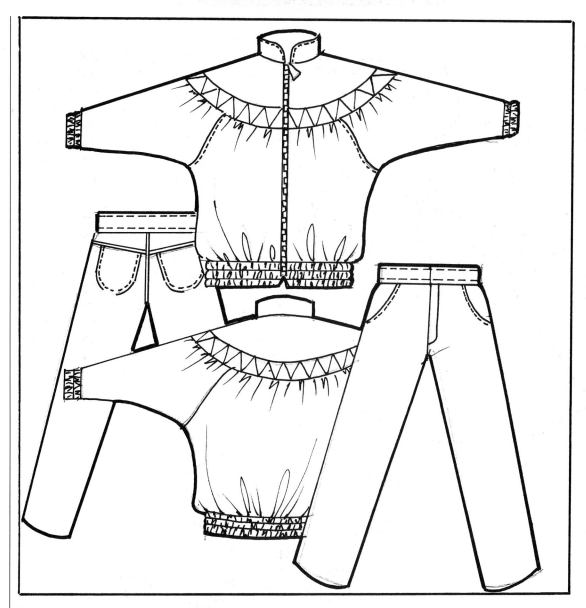

Casual jacket and trousers, back and
front view with detailed drawings for
the yoke and elasticated waistband.
Note the balance of the yoke, sleeves
and collar. The drawing was produced
with two pens of different line values;
a Pilot V ballpoint for the thin line,
and a Pentel sign pen for the thick
line.

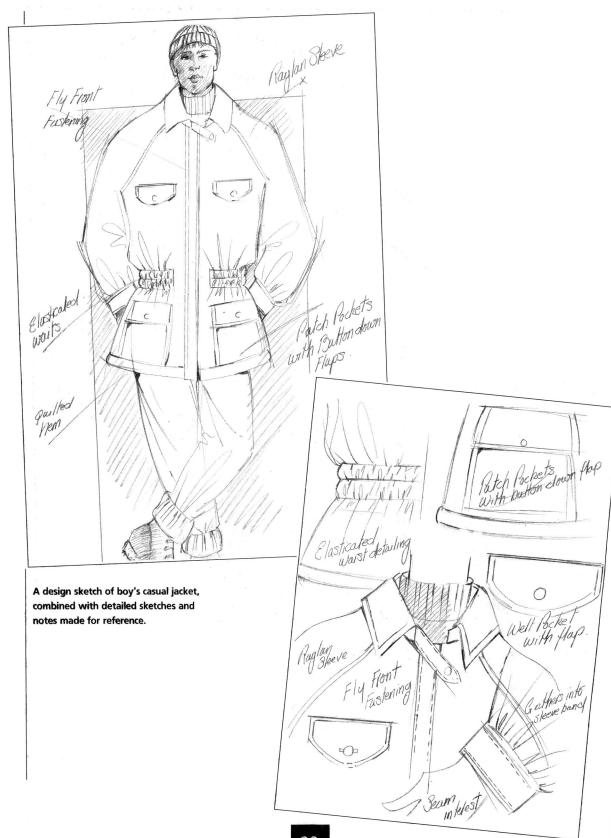

Fly Front Fastening

Raglan Sleeve

Elasticated waits

Quilted Hem

Patch Pockets with Button down Flaps

Patch Pockets with button down Flap

Elasticated waist detailing

Well Pocket with Flap

Raglan Sleeve

Fly Front Fastening

Gathers into sleeve band

Seam interest

A design sketch of boy's casual jacket, combined with detailed sketches and notes made for reference.

This working drawing illustrates the back and front view. Note the attention to the detail of the pockets, collar cuffs and elasticated bands at the waist.

Design development sheets illustrate a collection of design ideas based round a theme. The designer will produce a series of sketches before selecting the designs to develop for a collection. The sheets would illustrate front and back views, together with detail sketches, notes and sample fabrics.

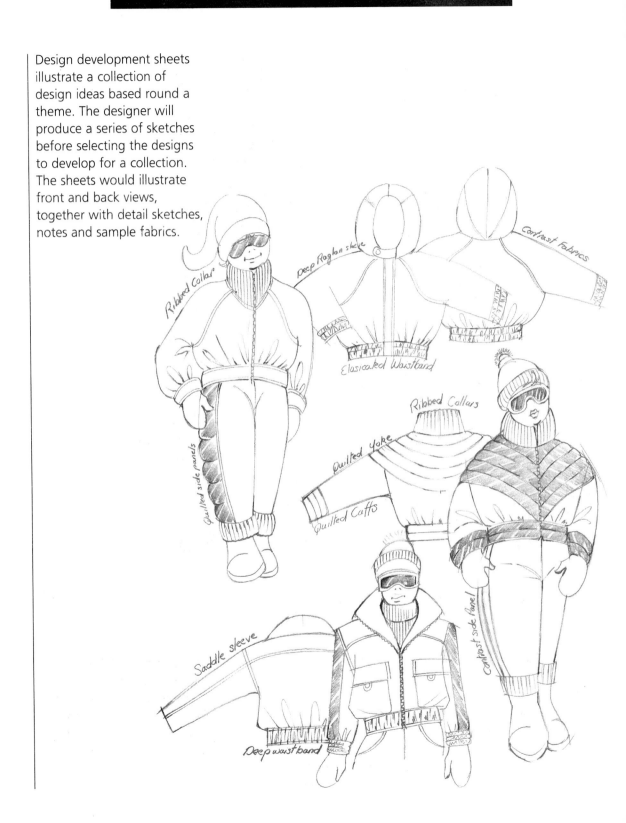

AUTUMN WINTER '95

Presentation drawings are used to promote a design collection. The drawings are made a standard size, which means that it is easier to handle them and send them by post.

The presentation should reflect the complete look, together with back view. It may be a working flat drawing or a figure. Often lettering and a background are added to project the mood and theme.

This type of work is helpful when the work of a student is assessed, as it gives a clear idea of how the ideas are developed and the effect of the final presentation.

Photocopiers

The photocopier is an invaluable tool for the fashion design illustrator. The photocopier can be used to:

1 enlarge and reduce drawings
2 reproduce drawings on which to experiment with colour, pattern and texture techniques before working on the original
3 produce material for background effects on presentation boards
4 transfer drawings on to different coloured papers
5 transfer drawings and photographs on to acetate, which is very effective for presentation work
6 paste-up drawings when working on the arrangement of design work. Cut out the figures and general artwork, and use spraymount to fix it on to clean white card. Photocopy in black and white or colour for a clean, professional look
7 photocopy artwork for reference when sending your originals off for competitions, etc
8 photocopy reference work when researching and collecting material for sketchbooks and storyboards
9 enlarge sections of design drawings, details of collars, pockets and other style features
10 photocopy textured and patterned materials, reducing the size to match the scale of the drawing when using a collage technique, or to apply paper to the drawing
11 photocopy airbrush effects for backgrounds, then use spraymount to attach your artwork on to it.

Marker pens

Marker pens are available in a wide range of colours and sizes, with many different nib sizes, from cylinder-shaped heads, blunt bullet-like points, wedge shapes and fine points. The inks are either water-soluble or spirit-based. Markers can be used for filling in areas of colour or for making bold outlines, to give a clean and pleasing effect. They are extremely convenient as they dry rapidly and are especially noted for their clarity of colour.

Pastels

Although no brushes are used, the use of pastels is more akin to painting than drawing – the advantage being that there is no liquid and hence no drying time to consider. The range of tints in each colour is considerable. A variety of tones can be achieved by treating the tinted paper as a mid-tone, and a coloured paper may be used as a key for the rest of the colour scheme. Different effects can be created, depending on which part of the pastel stick is used.

Watercolour

Watercolours may be bought as solid tablets or as paste in tubes, thinned with water before use. Paintboxes of different sizes are easily available. Paintbrushes vary in quality from sable to nylon. The paper surface is important. Unless you are using good quality paper, it should be stretched. If this is not done, the paper will react to the water by cockling, and your work will be distorted.

Gouache

Gouache is basically the same as watercolour, but it is mixed with white pigment which makes it opaque. When dry, gouache forms a positive film of colour. It is associated with hard divisions of solid colour. A free style of painting may also be achieved where the brush strokes are visible, working with wet paint on wet paper. Watercolour paper or boards are most suitable for gouache. Cartridge and layout papers are not suitable.

Coloured pencils

A wide range of coloured pencils is available, graded from very hard to extra soft. Pencils offer the most versatile method of colouring a drawing. By varying the pressure, different tone values may be obtained.

Water-soluble pencils are available in a wide colour range. To use them, the drawing is produced as normal, and then a watercolour wash is applied to produce an even colour, obliterating the pencil marks.

Wax and water-solvent crayons

A large selection of wax crayons in differing thicknesses is available. A solid, bright colour can be produced, and the harder the pressure, the deeper the tone. Some crayons are wax-based, which enables you to scratch into them for surface and texture effects. Others are water-based, and may be used combined with water.

Inks

Pen and ink creates immediate visual effects in both line and tone, which may take the form of lines, dots, hatching and cross hatching. Ink drawings combined with washes of coloured inks are most effective. Many different colours are available. Inks can either be used on their own, mixed together or diluted with water.

Wax-resistant effects

A wax crayon or candle may be used as a resistant to watercolour and inks. Firstly, mark the paper with the candle or crayon. The marked area will then repel the water based solutions. Therefore, when a wash is added, the area will remain free of colour. A rubber solution produces a similar effect.

Light box

A box used for tracing which has a glass top and contains a light. When the work to be traced is placed under a sheet of a paper resting on the glass, it is illuminated by the light below and it is shown clearly. These boxes are available in a range of sizes.

Airbrush

The airbrush provides perfect even tones, graded tones and soft lines. It will also blend colour. It is operated by a motor compressor or compressed air propellant aerosols.

Layout paper

White layout detail paper has a surface ideal for ink and pencil working. The paper is semi-transparent, which is useful when working over roughs and developing work.

BOOK LIST

FASHION ILLUSTRATION

Barnes, Colin, *Fashion Illustration*, Macdonald, 1988

Drake, Nicholas, *Fashion Illustration Today*, Thames and Hudson, 1987

Ireland, Patrick John, *Fashion Design*, Cambridge University Press, 1987

Ireland, Patrick John, *Fashion Design Drawing and Illustration*, Batsford, 1982

Ireland, Patrick John, *Fashion Design Illustration, Women*, Batsford, 1993

Ireland, Patrick John, *Encylopedia of Fashion Details*, Batsford, 1987, 1989

Kumager, Kojiro, *Fashion Illustrations*, Graphic-Sha, 1988

Parker, William, *Fashion Drawing in Vogue*, Thames & Hudson, 1983

Yajima, Isao, *Figure Drawing for Fashion*, Graphic-Sha, 1990

Yajima, Isao, *Mode Drawing*, Graphic-Sha, 1989

FIGURE DRAWING

Croney, John, *Drawing Figure Movement*, Batsford, 1983

Everett, Felicity, *Fashion Design*, Usborne, 1987

Gordon, Louise, *Anatomy and Figure Drawing*, Batsford, 1988

Loomis, Andrew, *Figure Drawing for all it's Worth*, Viking Press, 1971

Smith, Stan and Wheeler, Linda, *Drawing and Painting the Figure*, Phaidon, 1983

GRAPHICS

Dalley, Terence (Consultant Editor), *The Complete Guide to Illustration and Design Techniques and Materials*, Phaidon, 1980

Laing, J. and Davis, R. S., *Graphic Tools and Techniques*, Blandford Press, 1986

Lewis, Brian, *An Introduction to Illustration*, The Apple Press, 1987

Welling, Richard, *Drawing with Markers*, Pitman, 1974

HISTORY OF FASHION

Blum, Stella, *Designs by Erté*, Dover Publications, New York, 1976

Boucher, Francis, *A History of Costume in the West*, Thames & Hudson 1966

Davenport, Millia, *The Book of Costume*, Crown, New York, 1976

Ewing, Elizabeth and Mackrell, Alice, *History of Twentieth Century Fashion*, Batsford, new edition, 1992

Milbank, Caroline Reynolds, *Couture – the Great Fashion Designers*, Thames & Hudson, 1985

Murray, Maggie Pexton, *Changing Styles in Fashion*, Fairchild Publications, New York, 1989

O'Hara, Georgina, *The Encyclopedia of Fashion*, Thames & Hudson, 1986

Peacock, John, *The Chronicle of Western Costume*, Thames & Hudson, 1991

Stegmeyer, Anne, *Who's Who in Fashion*, Fairchild, 1988

Tilke, Max, *Costume Patterns and Design*, Magna Books, 1990